W9-BCI-653

613.7
ROY

Royston, Angela
Get some exercise!

$25.36
BC#34880000025341

DATE DUE	BORROWER'S NAME
9/15/09	

Look After Yourself

Get Some Exercise!

Angela Royston

Heinemann Library
Chicago, Illinois

Designed by Dave Oakley
Photo research by Helen Reilly
Originated by Dot Gradations Ltd
Printed and bound in China by South China Printing Company

07 06 05
10 9 8 7 6 5 4 3

Library of Congress Cataloging-in-Publication Data
Royston, Angela.
  Get some exercise! / Angela Royston.
      v. cm. -- (Look after yourself)
Includes bibliographical references and index.
Contents: Your body -- Your muscles -- A healthy heart -- Huff and puff -- Are you a couch potato? -- Walk, don't drive -- Move those muscles! -- Swim as often as you can -- Bend your joints -- Make your body stronger -- Play ball games-- Warming up and cooling down - It's a fact!
  ISBN 1-4034-4440-4 (libr. bdg.) -- ISBN 1-4034-4449-8 (pbk.)
  1. Exercise--Juvenile literature. [1. Exercise. 2. Physical fitness.]
I. Title.
  RA781.R698 2003
  613.7'1--dc21
                          2003000991

Acknowledgments
The author and publisher are grateful to the following for permission to reproduce copyright material:
Cover photograph by Lori Adamski-Peek.
pp. 4, 5 Arthur Tilley/Getty Images; pp 6, 7, 9, 12, 13, 26, 27 Trevor Clifford; p. 8 Jacob Tapeschaner/Getty Images; p. 10 Lori Adamski Peek/Getty Images; p. 11 Jade Albert Studios Inc/Getty Images; p. 14 Powerstock; p. 15 Simon Wilkinson/Getty Images; p. 16 Chad Slattery/Getty Images; p. 17 Jo Makin/Last Resort; p. 18 Zac Macauley/Getty Images; p. 19 Peter Cade/Getty Images; p. 20 Steve Lewis/Getty Images; pp. 21, 22, 24, 24 Alamy; p.23 Zac Macauley/Image Bank.

Special thanks to David Wright for his help in the preparation of this book.

Every effort has been made to contact copyright holders of any material reproduced in this book. Any omissions will be rectified in subsequent printings if notice is given to the publisher.

Some words are shown in bold, **like this.** You can find out what they mean by looking in the glossary.

Contents

Your Body

Running seems an easy thing to do, but it is not as simple as it seems. When you run, you use many **muscles** to move your legs.

Your muscles need **oxygen** to work. You breathe in oxygen when you breathe in air. Exercise helps your muscles work better.

Your Muscles

Muscles are part of the soft **flesh** that covers your bones. Bend your elbow and clench your fist. Now you can feel the muscles tighten in your arm.
A muscle tightens when it **contracts.**

Most muscles are attached to bones.
One end of the muscle in your
thigh is attached to your
shin bone. When this
muscle contracts, it
bends your knee.

thigh

shin

A Healthy Heart

Muscles use **oxygen** as they work. Oxygen from the air you breathe goes into your blood. Your **heart** brings this oxygen to your muscles.

As your heart beats, it pumps blood around your body. The more oxygen your muscles use, the faster your heart beats and the faster you breathe in.

Huff and Puff

Every day, try to do some exercise that makes you huff and puff. Running hard makes you breathe hard. This exercises your **heart** and **lungs.**

Dancing or skating can make you huff and puff, too. Breathing hard makes your lungs and heart work harder. Your **muscles** also become better at using **oxygen.**

11

Are You a Couch Potato?

Couch potatoes spend all day playing computer games or watching television. Without exercise, people become **unfit.** Their **hearts** and **lungs** will not work so well.

When someone who is unfit runs around, he or she quickly runs out of breath. Regular exercise makes your heart work better, so it does not have to work as hard to bring **oxygen** to your **muscles.**

Walk, Don't Ride

Walking is good exercise. It makes you breathe more deeply. This makes your **brain** work better, too.

14

If it is safe, walk to where you are going.
It may be more comfortable to travel by car,
but walking is better for your health!

Move Those Muscles!

Taking an elevator or an **escalator** is an easy way to go up several floors. Climbing stairs is harder work, but it exercises your **muscles, heart,** and **lungs.**

16

You can get lots of exercise by doing every-day things. Helping with the housework means lots of bending and stretching. That's good exercise!

Swim as Often as You Can

Some exercise uses only a few **muscles.** But swimming exercises all your muscles at the same time.

The muscles in your arms, legs, **stomach,** and chest move you through the water. Taking in deep breaths exercises your **lungs** and **heart.**

19

The parts of your body where your bones meet are called **joints.** Climbing keeps your joints and your **muscles** moving smoothly.

Dancing and sports like **judo** are good exercise for your muscles and joints. They help you control your muscles and keep your **balance.**

Make Your Body Stronger

Exercise makes your body stronger. Stretching your **joints** helps you to move better. Putting your weight on your bones makes them grow stronger.

The more you use your **muscles,** the stronger they become. Strong muscles help you move faster and farther than weak muscles.

Play Ball Games

Playing basketball or baseball helps you control your **muscles** and **joints.** You use muscles in your arms, shoulders, and back to throw a ball.

24

When you kick a ball, you use many different muscles in your legs and **stomach.** The more you practice kicking and throwing a ball, the stronger these muscles become.

Warming up and Cooling Down

You should stretch your body before you start to exercise. Stretching helps warm up your **muscles.** It also makes your **joints** move more easily.

When you have finished exercising, you should keep moving for a few minutes. Walk around or stretch some more. This will help **relax** your muscles and let them cool down.

It's a Fact!

When you are sitting quietly, your **heart** beats between 80 and 100 times a minute. When you exercise your heart beats faster—about 120 times a minute.

When your heart beats faster, it also pumps more blood with each beat. This means that more blood and **oxygen** reach your **muscles.**

When you are sitting quietly, each breath fills only about a quarter of your **lungs.** When you exercise, you breathe deeper and faster. You can take in more than ten times the air you take in when you are **relaxed.**

Your body needs oxygen to get **energy** from the food you eat.

When you exercise, your body becomes hotter and you **sweat.** Sweating helps you cool down. It also means that your body loses water. You should drink extra water when you exercise.

As people get older, their **joints** get stiffer. Children's joints work more smoothly than adults' joints. Exercising your joints helps stop them from becoming stiff.

Bread, spaghetti, rice, and potatoes are **starchy** foods. Your body needs these to make energy. Meat, eggs, cheese, and fish are foods that your body needs to build strong muscles.

Glossary

balance   keeping a steady position without falling over

brain   part of the body that controls the whole body and allows you to be aware of things

contract   to tighten and become shorter to move part of the body

energy   power to do work or move about

escalator   moving stairway that carries people from one floor to a higher or lower floor

flesh   soft substance that lies between your bones and your skin

heart   part of the body that pumps blood around

joint   part of the body where two or more bones meet. Joints allow you to bend and move different parts of your body.

judo   sport that practices self-defense

lung   part of the body that takes in oxygen from the air you breathe in

muscle   part of the body that tightens, or contracts, to move a bone or other part of the body

oxygen gas that all living things need to breathe in to stay alive. Oxygen is one of the gases in the air.

relax rest your body and mind

shin bone at the front of your lower leg. It joins your knee to your ankle.

starchy made of a substance that gives the body energy

stomach part of the body into which your food goes when you have swallowed it. Your stomach muscles are over your waist.

sweat salty water that the body makes in the skin, particularly when you are too hot

thigh part of the leg between the knee and the hip

unfit when a person's muscles, joints, heart, and lungs do not work as well as they should

More Books to Read

Gordon, Sharon. *Exercise*. Danbury, Conn.: Children's Press, 2002.

Royston, Angela. *A Healthy Body*. Chicago: Heinemann Library, 1999.

Vogel, Elizabeth. *Let's Exercise*. New York: PowerKids Press, 2001.

Index